Contents

The Filthy Streets of London

In 1665 London was a growing city. Its streets were crammed with houses, shops and businesses. With so many people, London was getting dirty and smelly. People threw all their waste on to the street or into the River Thames. And when they drank and washed with the dirty water from the Thames they often became ill.

Beginning History

THE PLAGUE

Stuarts + Tudors

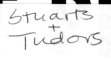

...jerly

...dam Hook

739.96

Text copyright © 2002 Hodder Wayland
Illustrations copyright © 2002 Adam Hook

Project manager: Louisa Sladen
Designer: Peta Morey

Published in 2002 by Hodder Wayland,
an imprint of Hodder Children's Books

British Library Cataloguing in Publication Data
Gogerly, Liz
The Plague. - (Beginning History)
1. Plague - England - History - 17th century - Juvenile literature
I. Title
614.5'732'00942'09032

ISBN 0 7502 3788 0

Printed and bound in Hong Kong

Hodder Children's Books
A division of Hodder Headline Limited
338 Euston Road, London NW1 3BH

Picture Acknowledgements
The publishers would like to thank the following for allowing their pictures to be
reproduced in this publication: Private Collection/Bridgeman Art Library 3, 5, 8,
16, City of Westminster Archive Centre, London/Bridgeman Art Library 10,
National Portrait Gallery, London/Bridgeman Art Library 13; Mary Evans Picture
Library *back cover, title page*, 6, 9 (top and bottom); OSF/Robin Redfern 7 (top),
OSF/G.I. Bernard 7 (bottom); Peter Newark Picture Library 19;
Museum of London 12; Popperfoto/Raveendran 21; Hodder Wayland Picture
Library 11, 12, 15 (top and bottom), 21, 23.

While every effort has been made to secure permission, in some cases it has
proved impossible to trace copyright holders.

The city of London was ▶
so overcrowded that
people even built houses
on London Bridge.

A woman throws
rubbish out of her
window and straight
into the river below!
▼

Many rich people built houses in the suburbs where it was cleaner. Meanwhile the poor crowded into filthy streets where it was easy to catch diseases. Londoners were used to smallpox, typhus and other terrible illnesses. But they didn't know that the common black rats that lived on their doorsteps were carrying the most feared disease of all – the plague.

'The Poor's Plague'

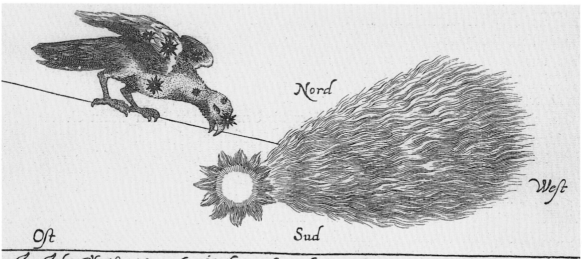

Im Jahr Christi. 1664. den $\frac{14}{24}$ Decemb: in der Nacht gegen Tag. nacht 5. der Klein-
nern Uhr. ward in deß H. Röm, Freyen Reichs Stadt Nürnberg, dieser
Erschröckliche Comet Stern wie hier Abgebildet zuersehen.

When the plague struck in 1665 nobody guessed that thousands of people would die. The first recorded case was in April. The victim was Margaret Ponteous who lived in a poor area of London called St Giles. The rich people were not surprised that it started there. They thought God was punishing the poor for their sins and they called it 'The Poor's Plague'.

▲ In 1664 and 1665 people saw comets in the night sky. They believed that this was a sign that something bad was about to happen.

The plague started in poorer areas because the black rats could always find something to eat among the rubbish thrown into the streets. These same rats were infested with fleas. The rats' fleas carried the plague virus.

Once a flea bit a person they would catch the plague. Once infected, people could pass the plague on through coughs and sneezes.

Many Londoners kept pigs and chickens in their gardens. The food they fed these animals and birds made a tasty meal for the black rat as well.
▼

◄ It isn't easy to see a flea as it jumps from person to person. But, if you look under a microscope, you can see how they look. This flea is biting a rabbit.

A Foul Disease

The plague was a horrible disease. The first symptoms were shivering, sweating, aching, vomiting and coughing blood. Next came diarrhoea, fever and confusion as the patient slipped in and out of sleep. Finally came sores and boils called *buboes*. Death followed quickly.

These doctors are looking at the body of a dead plague victim. Can you see the plague boils on the body?
▼

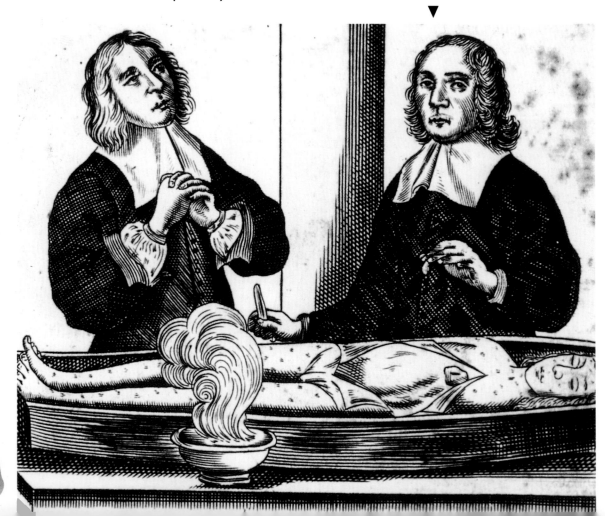

▲ Doctors dressed in special clothes and wore masks to try to protect themselves from catching the plague.

London's hospitals were soon overcrowded. Most of London's doctors escaped to the country, so patients were left in the hands of plague nurses. These old women didn't care for their patients properly. Sometimes, they would even murder their patients so they could steal their possessions.

Other people tried to cure themselves by taking herbs or magic potions. But, no matter what people did, there was no cure for the plague.

People tried to find cures for the plague. This man is taking a medicine he has made himself. Some people even tried magic spells as a cure. ►

A Red Cross Over the Door

Samuel Pepys lived in London during the plague. He kept a diary. In June he wrote: 'I did in Drury Lane see two or three houses marked with a red cross upon the doors.' A red cross on a door meant that somebody in that household had the plague. Nobody from that house was allowed to leave for 40 days – even if they didn't have the plague. Watchmen made sure that people obeyed these quarantine laws.

Samuel Pepys stayed in London in 1665, but he sent his wife away to the countryside where she would be safe.
▼

By the middle of June, 1,000 people were dying from the plague each week. Richer people, including merchants, doctors and churchmen, fled to their homes in the country.

◄ Some people managed to leave London by boat. Others had to go by horse or even on foot.

Many people tried to break the quarantine laws. Some gave the watchmen money to let their healthy children leave the infected household.

▼

Taking Action

Laws were introduced to stop the plague from spreading. Nobody understood how the plague spread, but visitors to London were ordered to leave and the gates of London were closed. Theatres and shops were closed down. Over 40,000 cats and dogs were killed in case they were spreading the disease. But this made the situation worse. Now the black rat had no enemies.

When Londoners killed thousands of dogs and cats they made life easier for the black rat. Now, it had lots more food to eat.

▼

During the plague, the Mayor of London passed new laws. One of these was that all the schools had to be closed until the plague had gone!

▼

To the Alderman of the Ward of

By the Mayor.

The rest of Britain took action too. Many cities, towns and villages were closed to visitors. Some people even burned letters which came from London in case they carried the plague. Londoners looked towards King Charles II for help, but in July he left for Salisbury – Londoners were on their own.

▲ **Many poor people were angry with King Charles II. They thought he should have stayed in London to help at this difficult time.**

'Bring Out Your Dead!'

By August over 7,000 people were dying each week. Shouts of 'Bring out your dead!' and the ringing of handbells when the dead carts arrived were the loudest sounds in the empty city.

▲ These gravediggers are working at night. But soon gravediggers would have to work during the day too.

◄ A deathly sound! The ring of a handbell meant that the dead cart was near.

The dead carts took the corpses away to be buried. But the bodies were piling up so quickly it was impossible to bury them before they began to rot. The stench from the graveyards was terrible. As the graveyards filled up, mass graves were dug on open ground. Before the plague, it was the custom to bury the dead at night. Now the dead had to be buried during the day too.

▲ Large graves were dug so that many plague victims could be buried at the same time.

The Ghost Town

London became like a ghost town. Shops, theatres and all public places had been shut for months. Weeds and rubbish had grown up in the parks, streets and the King's palace. People ignored the quarantine laws too. In his diary Samuel Pepys wrote: 'But Lord, how empty the streets are, and melancholy, so many poor sick people in the streets, full of sores, and so many sad stories overheard as I walk...'

London was no longer ▶ the lively city it had been. Plague victims wandered the empty streets.

This book shows what people died from in London in one week in 1665. You can see that 3,880 people died from the plague. One poor person even died of fright!

▼

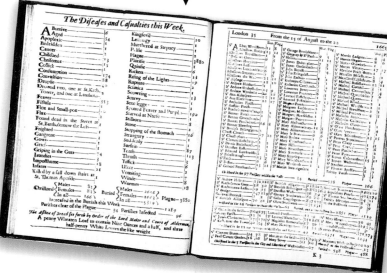

Fortunately in December the number of people dying started to fall. Gradually life returned to normal. In February 1666, King Charles II returned. To celebrate his return, the bells rang out over the city.

The Plague Disappears

Nobody knows for sure how many people died from the plague. People called 'searchers of the dead' counted the corpses and recorded nearly 70,000 deaths. No one knows why the plague disappeared either. After the 1670s there have been no cases in Britain.

We will never know how many people really died from the plague because the searchers of the dead were sometimes paid to report other causes of death.

▼

▲ During the Great Fire of London, people were forced to flee London once again. But luckily only nine people died during the fire.

Some people say that the Great Fire of London in September 1666 helped to clear away the plague for good. Others say that people had become stronger after being exposed to the plague and that they had grown immune to the disease. But perhaps it's because the black rat died out, and the brown rat that replaced it didn't carry the plague.

'Ring-A Ring O' Roses'

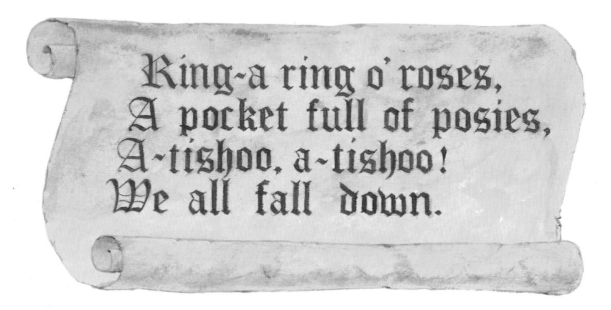

Ring-a ring o' roses,
A pocket full of posies,
A-tishoo, a-tishoo!
We all fall down.

Although the great plague happened a long time ago, children still sing about it. The popular nursery rhyme 'Ring-A Ring O' Roses' goes back to 1665. The 'ring o' roses' is the red rash that plague victims got on their bodies. The 'pocket full of posies' are the flowers and herbs that people tried to use as a cure. 'A-tishoo, a-tishoo!' are the sneezes which passed the plague on. And 'We all fall down' is the death of the poor plague victims.

The plague had been ▶ so terrible that people feared its return. The skeleton in this picture is a symbol of death. It reminds people that the plague might come back.

In 1994, the plague returned, in India. It had killed thousands of people there. Luckily, modern medicines called antibiotics cured new victims. At last, doctors could stop the disease that once killed so many of us.

▲ A modern-day plague victim.

Glossary

Antibiotics Drugs which are used to cure infections or diseases.

Confusion When a person doesn't know what they are doing or saying.

Corpses Dead bodies.

Crammed Lots of things fitted in a small space.

Custom Something that is usually done – a tradition.

Immune Protected against a disease or illness, often by an injection. But sometimes people's bodies can create their own protection.

Mass graves A lot of corpses piled into one big grave.

Melancholy To be very sad.

Posies A bunch of flowers or herbs.

Possessions Things which belong to a person.

Quarantine When an animal or person is kept apart from others, in order to stop a disease from spreading.

Sins The bad things that people do, such as telling lies or stealing.

Smallpox One of the most dangerous diseases of the seventeenth and eighteenth centuries. Victims would experience fever and get spots which left terrible scars.

Stench A dreadful smell.

Suburbs An area of houses at the edge of a town or city.

Symptoms Something that is wrong with you that shows you have an illness. A running nose is one of the symptoms of a cold.

Typhus A disease which is usually associated with dirty and overcrowded living conditions. Victims would experience headaches and fever.

Virus Tiny little organisms which multiply in the body to cause disease.

Vomiting Being sick.

Watchmen People who were employed to make sure people didn't enter or leave a building where people were infected with the plague.

Further Information

Books to Read

All About the Great Plague by Pam Robson (Hodder Wayland, 1996, 2002)

Great Plague and Fire by Richard Tames (Heinemann, 1999)

Websites You Can Visit

Read about the plague in extracts from Samuel Pepys' diary.
www.usd.edu/~jwortham/ chough/plague.html

An overview of the plague with some tasks for school children.
atschool.eduweb.co.uk/ heathsid/Subjects/History/ plague.htm

Places to Visit

The Museum of London, London Wall, London EC2
(Telephone 020 7600 3699; website: info@museumoflondon.org.uk) – you can see old papers from 1665 which show the names of people who died in London. Next to each name is a description of what they died from. You will see that most deaths that year were from the plague.

Index